D1046748

Busy Buzzing Bumblebees

and Other Tongue Twisters

by Alvin Schwartz

illustrated by

Kathie Abrams

An I CAN READ Book®

Harper & Row, Publishers

Busy Buzzing Bumblebees and Other Tongue Twisters
Text copyright © 1982 by Alvin Schwartz
Illustrations copyright © 1982 by Kathie Abrams
All rights reserved. No part of this book may be
used or reproduced in any manner whatsoever without
written permission except in the case of brief quotations
embodied in critical articles and reviews. Printed in
the United States of America. For information address
Harper & Row, Publishers, Inc., 10 East 53rd Street,
New York, N.Y. 10022. Published simultaneously in
Canada by Fitzhenry & Whiteside Limited, Toronto.

First Edition

Library of Congress Cataloging in Publication Data
Schwartz, Alvin, date
    Busy buzzing bumblebees and other tongue twisters.

    (An I can read book)
    Summary: A collection of forty-six tongue twisters.
    1. Tongue twisters. [1. Tongue twisters]
I. Abrams, Kathie, ill. II. Title. III. Series.
PN6371.5.S38   818'.5402   81-48639
ISBN 0-06-025268-5   AACR2
ISBN 0-06-025269-3 (lib. bdg.)

For Barbara, Betsy, and Nan

A tongue twister

will twist your tongue

and make you laugh.

Just say it three times

as fast as you can.

Flash message!

Six sharp smart sharks!

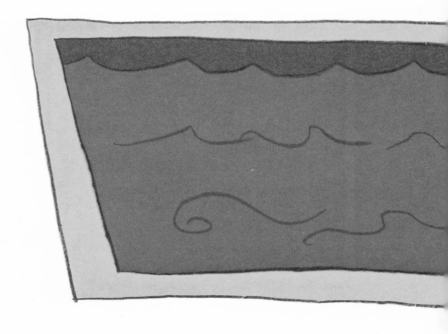

Swim, Sam! Swim, Sam! Swim, Sam!

Well swum, Sam!

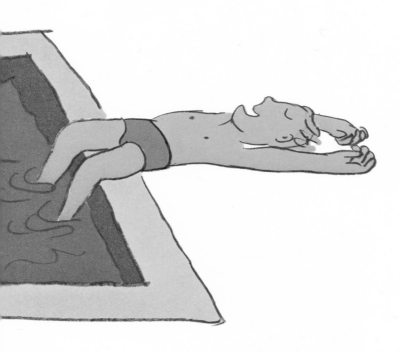

Six sticky sucker sticks.

Eight gray geese.

Nine nice night nurses nursing nicely.

13

Sixty-six sneaky snakes.

Tom Knott knits

knitted knotted knots.

If Stu chews shoes,

should Stu choose

the shoes he chews?

Big Bill blew big blue bubbles.

Down the slippery slide

slid Sam.

Which witch watched which watch?

21

She sells seashells

by the seashore.

The black back brake broke.

23

Danger!

Deep damp dark

dirty deadly dismal dungeon!

To toot and to hoot!

To hoot and to toot!

Ruth's wet red roof.

Polly Pobble's

pot of pebbles.

Blue booties are beauties.

A proper copper coffeepot.

Tillie's twin thin sister.

Big Ben Blimber.

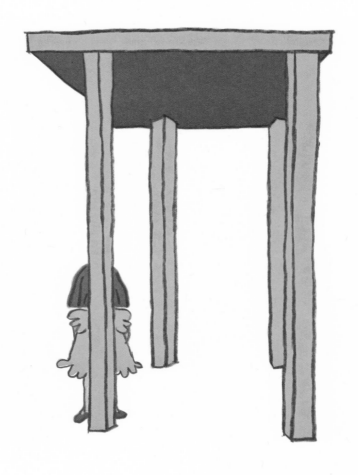

Shy sly Sheila.

Sam Short thought

Sara Smith so sweet.

Nellie Needle nibbles noodles.

Peter pared the peel

from the pile of pears

in the pail.

Ron rolled a round roll

around a round room.

Crispy crusty crunchy crunch.

"This bun is better buttered,"

Billy muttered.

Blake the baker

bakes black bread.

Pete's pop shops

for chops

in chop shops.

Cheap sheep soup.

Fresh fruit float.

The big book crook

took the big cookbook.

47

On a light night,

I don't need

a night-light.

Did the butterfly

flutter by

the butterfly?

Five fat frogs fled from

fifty fierce fish.

A big black bug

bit a big black bear.

Crickets chirp in thickets.

There is a spider

inside the cider

beside her.

Busy buzzing bumblebees
buzzing busily.

A picky pet pig

picked a pine pigpen.

Hiccup teacup.

When you have the hiccups,

take a breath,

and try this twister.

And your hiccups may go away.

How high would a horsefly fly

if a horsefly

would fly high?

How much dew

would a dewdrop drop,

if a dewdrop did drop dew?

Crow, Cock!

Caw, Crow!

People all over the world use tongue twisters. They tell them in French and Chinese and all the other languages.

Some of these twisters are very old. The famous "Peter Piper picked a peck of pickled peppers" twister and others started out in England over three hundred years ago.

But there also are twisters that are brand-new, like "Crispy crusty crunchy crunch" and "Cheap sheep soup." It is fun to make them up.

You can make up a twister of your own. Just think of a sentence in which all the words start with the same letter or sound. And you will twist a tongue.

Alvin Schwartz